What is Creation Centred Spirituality?

GreenSpirit

GreenSpirit, the Association for Creation Spirituality in Britain, is part of a widespread movement exploring different ways of seeing, and living in, our world. More and more people are realising that we cannot continue using the earth and her creatures as if we owned them, increasing the gap between the haves and the have-nots in society, and despoiling the earth.

New insights from ecology, psychology and the physical sciences, linking the latest Western knowledge and understanding to traditional wisdom, can lead us to a different way of perceiving our presence on earth. We need a profound shift in thinking and feeling to convert the present over-consumption to a simpler, more compassionate way of living here.

GreenSpirit Pamphlets

Each GreenSpirit pamphlet expresses the views of its author, which are not necessarily representative of the Association of Creation Spirituality as a whole.

1. Rediscovering St Francis: Earth Wisdom for the New Millennium.
    Alan José, 1998.

2. What's Radical Now? Politics and Creation Spirituality.
    Victor Anderson, 1998.

3. The New Universe Story.
    Michael Colebrook, 1998.

4. What is Creation Centred Spirituality?
    Grace Blindell, 2001.

5. Walking the Sacred Story. A New Ritual for Celebrating the Universe.
    Erna & Michael Colebrook, 2000.

Distributed By

GreenSpirit Books,
14 Beckford Close, Warminster, Wilts BA12 9LW.
http://www.greenspirit.org/books

What is Creation Centred Spirituality?

Grace Blindell

Illustrations by Marie Allen

London
Association for Creation Spirituality
2001

Published by the Association for Creation Spirituality.
Centre for Creation Spirituality, St James's Church, 197 Piccadilly,
London W1J 9LL
Regd. Charity No. 1045532
© Association for Creation Spirituality 2001

ISBN 0 9532551 5 8. 2nd revised edition
(ISBN 0 9532551 3 1. 1st edition)

Printed on recycled paper by Itchen Printers Limited, Southampton

For Andy, Jenny, Wook,
Sam, Tasman, Oscar and Rosa

CONTENTS

PREFACE.

Creation Spirituality is a tapestry woven of many strands, not least of which is the whole context of human cultural history, which, together with the insights of modern science, has revolutionalised our view of our place in the cosmos. Because of this it is not until the third chapter that the threads come together and the pattern emerges. The reader will find, therefore, that although Creation Spirituality is barely mentioned in the first two chapters yet it is upon the explorations and insights examined in these chapters that the vision of a Creation Centred Spirituality rests. All who read this pamphlet will be diverse in their needs, their expectations, as well as their insights, so although this work reflects one person's understanding and experience of this movement, it is sincerely hoped that, having reached the end, each reader will recognise their place within the wide embrace of Creation Spirituality.

ACKNOWLEDGEMENTS.

Very many thanks indeed are due to Regan von Schweitzer for her gift of non-stop encouragement during the writing of this pamphlet, to Marie Allen for her illustrations and to Josephine Teagle as well as Regan for their helpful and insightful criticisms. My thanks are also due to Chris Clarke for his very specific input in chapter 2, as well as for his valuable and helpful suggestions throughout. Finally to Petra Griffiths for supplying me with the historical data, and to Enid Bloomfield (of N.Z.) for one important reminder.

All poems in the text without specific attribution are by the Author.

The front cover, from *Tropical Storm with a Tiger (Surpris!)* by Henri Rousseau, is reproduced by permission of the National Gallery.

1. OUR JOURNEY IN UNDERSTANDING.

The land slips and slides
Creases and crumples,
From an old geological mind-set
To a new one.
The human spirit, standing on its own fault-line
Perceives the new horizon
Slowly. [1]

Throughout the brief span that the human species has been upon this beautiful planet our interpretation of our relationship with the natural world has shifted, both consciously and unconsciously. This relationship is with the animals, plants, trees, the elements of wind, water, air and earth, as well as the sun, moon and stars. Running parallel has been humankind's

[1] All poems in the text without specific attribution are by the Author.

developing and shifting attempts to define, explain and understand the great mystery of Creation itself.

It is with this broad sweep of human imagination faced with the mysterious and inexplicable that this first chapter is concerned. As we let our minds drift both back in historical time, and laterally within this present moment, we see an extraordinary panorama. We see tribal deities, concerned with a small group of people, we see pantheons of gods, each with their individual responsibilities. We see deities of place, mountain, river, sea, the sky. We see goddesses concerned with fertility and the seasons. We see a deep reverence for the natural world.

Slowly, not necessarily everywhere, we see shifts towards a single deity and the influence this had upon human attitudes. Concepts of justice as well as punishment, forgiveness as well as revenge, begin to be seen.

We are now aware of this slow evolution of human interpretation and explanation to ourselves of 'how things are'. Through the eyes of Creation Spirituality, no one step invalidates a previous awareness, although our human history is tragically marked by the false assumption that each new wider understanding must demolish all that went before.

The aim of this chapter is to put Creation Spirituality in its context within the natural progression of human awareness. As just highlighted in the previous paragraph, there is a danger here of our wanting to be the one true and final 'revelation', giving in to our human desire to 'be right' and to 'have the answer'. However, to take that stance would be to follow the old path to division and antagonism. One of the great 'certainties' that underlies the new, wider vision that inspires Creation Spirituality is its embrace of the Whole. Both the evolving human understanding together with the evolving natural world are seen as an ongoing but unfinished journey, our 'enlightenment' today a part of an ongoing and unfolding Universe. This in no way belittles any part of the journey; each understanding, each awareness a vital link in an evolving Whole. The new wider vision of Creation Spirituality must therefore be willing to accept both knowing and 'not knowing'.

To look at one example, we turn to humankind's view of the place of the sun. When it was postulated that the sun did not do what the evidence of our eyes told us that it did, but first that the earth was round and later that the earth rotated and orbited the sun, what a terrifying shift that demanded of our interpretation of our place within the visible Universe. Instead of the comfortable security of a flat earth, with God in (his) abode above, and hell and its domain below; the sun placed in the sky by God and journeying its everlasting 24 hour odyssey from east to west, then plunging through the dark underworld to reappear daily in the east; the stars fixed and permanent as a sort of back-drop; instead came this terrifying reversal of all that certainty. What must it have been like to have been at the centre of all that upheaval?

And yet... what really happened? We were simply being impelled towards a widening of our horizons. Nothing had really changed, our planet had been circling the sun for 4½ billion years, the earth had been revolving on its own axis for 4½ billion years. The change that was being demanded was a change in our human perceptions, an abandoning of the cosy security of the earlier Cosmology to something less clear-cut, more mysterious, wider, more awe-inspiring, but nevertheless a reality that had always been so.

A Cosmology is a belief system which defines the place of the human within the Cosmos.

We live in and are part of an evolving and ever-expanding Universe, and evolution is a continuous process. Nor is it the physical world alone which is in the process of change; this process includes also consciousness in all its forms.

Bede Griffiths (the Christian/Hindu mystic who died recently) on being asked: 'Is the Universe going somewhere?' replied, 'Yes, towards consciousness'. [2]

This first chapter has attempted to show, in a very generalised way, how the conscious awareness of the human race has moved, has shifted and changed, in an ongoing attempt to orient and define its place within, and its relationship with the perceived world in both its natural and sacred dimensions.

We do not need to be scientists, nor do we need to be cosmologists, but we do need to know our own human cosmic story. Only when we know that story do we begin to understand our place within it.

The next chapter will look at the changes and challenges that arose in the 20th century, and which continue to confront us.

2. THE CHALLENGE OF THE 20TH CENTURY... AND BEYOND.

> We simply have to explore the religious implications of Quantum Theory and the Big Bang origins of the Universe.
>
> Walter Schwarz. Former Religious Editor of the Guardian.

Creation Spirituality rests firmly upon the new understanding of the nature of reality that has emerged during the 20th century, and upon the subsequent shifts and movements that have developed in the light of this wider awareness.

In this chapter I invite you, the reader, to enter into a simple, but accurate, presentation of these new insights, and respond with your whole humanity — not only the intellect, but with your spirit, your emotions, and that deep instinctive 'knowing' which lies buried within our human species. To quote Lorna Marsden, a respected Quaker thinker:

> The spiritual life, the life of imagination and the heart is an endowment of humanity that is primal. It works against the elevation of the use of reason beyond the borders of reason's competence.[3]

Brian Swimme, in a lecture given at the Institute in Culture and Creation Spirituality at Oakland California, said this:

> We had the mind once to comprehend... we have drowned that in a pursuit of the knowledge of how/why, and now we have lost that ability, buried under words, numbers, measurements. We now have the story, but without the mind to comprehend fully... our technological mind is incapable of appropriating the news.

Creation Spirituality recognises this deep split that has been created within the human mind by our mechanical western pursuit of the how/why and seeks to heal that split. Not by going back,

---

[3] Lorna Marsden (1991) 'People and Planet, the Spiritual Dimension', *The Friend's Quarterly*, Nov 1991.

nor by denying the intellect, but by seeking a synthesis between these two equally needed parts of ourselves.

The two discoveries that have changed our understanding of the nature of the Universe and thus of who we are and our place within that Universe in a fundamental way are these:

Firstly what is loosely called 'the Big Bang' origin of the Universe, and secondly what is equally loosely referred to as Quantum Physics. To enter into the reality of the meaning of these revelations far more is required than the workings of the human brain. The human being possesses so much more — vision, imagination, intuition, as well as a deep shamanic quality to 'know'. These are our inheritance, and it is this quality of knowing that is evoked by the wonder of the new story.

As the 19th century faded and the 20th century dawned, we lived, or thought we did, against a backdrop of an unchanging and stable Universe. It is true that the idea of evolution — that is to say, of ongoing adaptation — had entered our consciousness, but that idea was exclusively confined to the biological world.

Yet within a few decades that stable and unchanging Universe had become an expanding and evolving one, and not only that, it had become a Universe with an identifiable beginning, and one that would finally end.

The new telescopes built through this last century, first on mountain tops and now launched on satellites, have seen further and further into space, observing events that happened longer and longer ago, from which the light is only now reaching us. We are seeing how, billions of years ago, the Universe was a frenzy of wild activity, galaxies colliding as they condensed from a maelstrom of turbulent gas; we are seeing how, billions of years before that, the earliest stages were completely calm, an almost featureless cloud of shining concentrated incandescence where only the tiniest ripples hinted at the creative emergence to come later. Theoretical calculations then take us further back still, over the 300,000 years of this cloud's lifetime, which our telescopes cannot penetrate, to the unimaginable earliest events that both brought forth the physical patterns that shape our material world, and also determined the precise chemical composition of that cloud, so crucial for the evolution to come. This is the 'Big Bang Theory', strangely named for such a calm and seemingly featureless beginning.

Nothing that the human species has had to comprehend in its brief span on this planet, compares with the challenge of this new revelation. We are the first generation of humans to know, at a concrete and factual level, the story of the Universe, and to face its implications — that this is also our own story. Nor is this new understanding some sort of optional extra that we can opt out of under the pretext 'I am not a scientist', 'I am not a cosmologist' or even 'I am not religious'. This vast all-embracing new understanding literally contains everything within its unfolding.

Here the same staggering new knowledge is being described by Brian Swimme and Thomas Berry in their book *The Universe Story*.

> ... a momentous change in human consciousness ... a change of such significance in its order of magnitude that we might think of it as revelatory, meaning by this term a new awareness of how the ultimate mysteries of existence are being manifested in the Universe about us.[4]

From that first primordial flaring forth until this present moment, every star that has been born and died, every whirling galaxy and every atom, every life form that has come and gone, every earthworm and every cabbage, all the great forests that have covered the planet, each unique sunrise and sunset, dance

---

[4] Brian Swimme and Thomas Berry (1992) *The Universe Story*, Harper San Francisco, Ch. 12, p. 223.

8

and rhythm, music, art and poetry, all human emotions, all human spirituality, the questioning human mind, the rise of consciousness — all, without exception, are an inseparable part of the ongoing story.

Ernesto Cardenal in his narrative poem *The Music of the Spheres* evokes the grandeur and the magic of the place of the human within this unfolding cosmos.

> Suppose reader, we want to see the star HD193182,
> The star could not see its beauty
> Unless we did.
> We are the star seeing itself.
> Born in its fire
> and cooled to be able to think and see.
> Protons, neutrons, and electrons
> are the human body, the planet, and the stars.
> From the unconscious consciousness came,
> So in us the planet loves and dreams.[5]

[5] Ernesto Cardenal (1990) *The Music of the Spheres*, trans. Dinah Livingstone, Katabase.

Yes, we are indeed not a separate species objectively surveying the Universe, but the Universe itself reflecting upon itself.

Yet we cannot hope to grasp the true depths of meaning within this story until we find again within ourselves that quality of imagination which is our human inheritance. Not lost... but overlaid with the deadening dust of undiluted mechanical science. In their book *The Universe Story* Brian Swimme and Thomas Berry warn against seeing only the scientific mechanistic story. They say:

> This story incorporates the human into the irreversible historical sequence of universal transformations. The important thing to appreciate is that this story... is not a story of a mechanistic, essentially meaningless universe but the story of a universe that has from the beginning had its mysterious self-organising power that, if experienced in any serious manner, must evoke an even greater sense of awe than that evoked in earlier times at the experience of dawn breaking over the hills, of the night sounds of the tropical rainforests, for it is out of this story that all of these phenomena have emerged.[6]

What about the second of these shifts in our understanding, Quantum Physics? In quantum physics we are no longer faced with the solid facts of Newtonian science which assumed that complete understanding of the nature of the physical world could be reached by reducing everything down to its smallest 'building blocks'. During the 20th century scientists have tried to do just that, following the simple theory that once we had broken down the elements of matter into their smallest particles then we should understand not only the nature of matter but the nature of the Universe itself.

Alas, the quest was like peeling layers from an onion, where each layer revealed a further one below, until the last 'ultimate layer', if such a thing there was, was seen to be far beyond the

---

[6] Swimme and Berry (1992) *op. cit.* Ch. 12, p. 238.

capabilities of experimentation to probe, even if the entire energy output of the earth was harnessed in the attempt. But in the course of this hunt came an apparent paradox. Even at the first stages of the onion peeling, when science uncovered the electrons that spray the pictures onto our television screens and the photons (particles of light) that are manipulated in the night-time viewing devices of the modern soldier, these objects — electrons, photons, and the many others later to join them — seemed sometimes to behave as particles, and sometimes as waves.

Dana Zohar, in her book *The Quantum Self* says:

> The most revolutionary statement that quantum physics makes about the nature of matter, and perhaps of being itself, follows from its description of the wave/particle duality, the assertion that all being at the sub-atomic level can be described equally well either as solid particles, like so many .billiard balls, or as waves, like undulations on the surface of the sea... it is the duality itself which is most basic. Quantum 'stuff' is essentially both wave-like and particle-like simultaneously.[7]

So the stuff of the Universe, the stuff of which we too are fashioned, is both solid and firm, possible to pinpoint in space, and at the same time, subtle, wave-like, rippling, interpenetrating, and impossible to pinpoint in space.

This coexistence of waves and particles was fully understood at the new intellectual level through work by the Cambridge physicist Paul Dirac in the 1940's. But the intellectual struggle is only one aspect of the challenge of quantum physics. As humans we are called to go beyond the intellectual, responding as well with that other part of ourselves, which can rise to transcend paradox and live wildly with mystery and uncertainty. It is that part of ourselves that knows what Schrödinger, one of the

---

[7] Danah Zohar (1990) *The Quantum Self,* Bloomsbury Publishing Ltd. Ch. 2, p. 9.

founders of quantum theory, called its greatest revelation: interconnectedness — a key concept — which I need to describe in a
little detail.

It was predicted in the 1930's but only experimentally verified
by the French physicist Alain Aspect in the 1980's. He carried
out experiments on pairs of photons (particles of light) which
were produced from a common source (a tube of fluorescent
dye) and which then travelled to opposite sides of the labora-
tory. He found a wonderful synthesis of freedom and related-
ness: the two particles responded unpredictably, but in a way
that was determined by whatever contexts they were placed in,
and in a way in which the two particles harmonised their free
responses. They behaved as if they continued to share a common source for their ongoing creativity.

What quantum theory presented in stark, unavoidable form, the
rest of science woke up to as something that had been over-
looked but was now obvious. Of course the whole universe is
interlinked by fields that never wholly fade, however far they
penetrate! Of course most systems are poised to respond unpredictably to the subtlest influence from the most distant star!
Of course! But how are we to respond to disclosures that challenge us to open up to the deeper intuitions of our hearts?

Charlene Spretnak in her book *States of Grace* pinpoints our dilemma very accurately (and amusingly) when she says:

> Insistent on avoiding any metaphorical mumbo-jumbo, so
> abhorrent to the modern mind... they (the scientists) seem
> to place their faith in declaring a directive to society that is
> almost charming in its naiveté. "Everything is composed of
> a subatomic flux of wavelets and particles, chaos and pat-
> tern, boundaries are fluid. Possibilities are endless. Unre-
> lated separateness is an illusion. Interconnectedness is real-
> ity. Process is all. Revise your perceptions, concepts, and
> life accordingly. Any questions?"

Just a few, Charlene Spretnak continues,

> Since modern socialisation has taught us to deny subtle per-
> ceptions that do not fit with a rationalist, mechanistic model
> of existence, how are we supposed to instantly develop our
> atrophied sensitivity in order to grow in awareness of the
> intricate, moment-to-moment dance of creation, disintegra-
> tion and recreation? [8]

A dilemma indeed — for we are (at present) out of balance, our
rational and intellectual side having been raised to the status of
final arbiter. How do we redress the balance?

> The shift into the New Story is just this... seeing differently.
> Matthew Fox.[9]

To say now that Creation Spirituality has the answer would be
to invite the reader to stop reading forthwith! But Creation
Spirituality does indeed acknowledge and embrace the prob-
lem...

How do we begin 'to see things differently'?

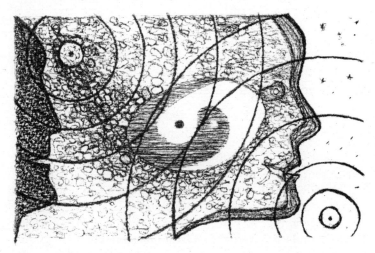

---

[8] Charlene Spretnak (1991) *States of Grace*, Harper San Francisco, Ch. 1,
p.21.
[9] Matthew Fox (1991) Lecture, The Institute in Culture and Creation Spirituality, Oakland, California.

TOWARDS SEEING DIFFERENTLY.

I shall lure myself into this new way
Slowly, subtly,
And with cunning.
I shall take myself by surprise
And trick myself towards
That teasing boundary
One way or another.
Too long have I lived
This side of the frontier
Kow-towing to the Single Straight Line,
Whilst over there
Flutter the many-dimensional
Butterflies of paradox.
I shall walk daily
Along that tremulous meridian
And learn . . .
I shall lay my ear
To the pulse-beat of the planet
And know. . .
I shall dwell
Within the inner and outer together
And see . . .
That my end is my beginning,
That all things are connected,
That there is no longer
I and Thou,
Nor I and It,
Only the One.

To end this chapter, let us look at those subtle shifts that are taking place today. The Quaker writer quoted earlier (Lorna Marsden, 1991) describes these changes as 'the opening of horizons towards the unification of knowledge'.

These movements can be seen as the breaking down of ancient barriers as well as the widening of narrowly held concepts, so that the separate and seemingly irreconcilable parts come together to make a balanced whole. I do not intend to examine these movements in detail, they come from different starting points and have a bewildering variety of names. However, they have two immensely important things in common. Firstly, they are grass-roots in their origins. Secondly, in every case they expose to the light previously divided — or even buried and denied — aspects of a whole. This coming together of hitherto opposed facets, this joining of polarities, is a profound indication of the compelling urge towards wholeness from which there can be no turning back.

These movements we now see all around us. The rise of feminism asserts the need for balance within a society predominately male dominated. Off-shoots of this embrace the retrieval of the feminine aspect of the Divine, the rediscovery of the Goddess, and last but by no means least it releases men from the stultifying impositions of patriarchy.

The revolution we see within medicine with the rapid spread of alternative approaches to healing which look beyond the symptoms to the context of the illness or complaint, is again indicative of the growing drive towards seeing the whole rather than the parts.

What is loosely described as the 'green' movement comprises a wide spectrum, and yet without exception it is grassroots in its origins. Greenpeace, Friends of the Earth, animal rights movements, the concern for organic farming, environmentalist movements, the concern for endangered species and for rain forests, Deep Ecology, one and all, and many more acknowledge our inter-connectedness and interdependence upon the planet.

Within the realm of psychology there is a trickle-down effect to more individual attempts to deepen our understanding of our own personalities and our 'shadow-sides'. Co-counselling, the Myers-Briggs system, the Enneagram, counselling, and psycho-synthesis, to name just a few.

The tentative rapprochement between the leading representa-tives of the various religions is only a shadowy reflection of the global spread of interest and cross-over taking place among or-dinary people. Without doubt this can be seen as an awakening of 'spirituality' at the expense of allegiance to a creed or guru.

The Quaker Universalist Group basis which states 'We believe that no one faith can claim to have a monopoly of the Truth' could perhaps sum up this more open approach.

Finally, and noticeably in those countries where a western colo-nial attitude has despised and belittled the native wisdoms and spiritualities, there has been a renaissance of those suppressed wisdoms. Parallel with this has been a recognition from the predominately western cultures that indigenous peoples have much to teach us, and that learning is a two-way process.

As mentioned earlier, it is not my purpose to list and explain every one of these movements, rather it is to alert the reader to the global phenomenon, the paradigm shift that is actually un-der way, and to the holistic vision which lies behind each frag-ment of this mosaic. Within the wider view, it can be seen that, consciously or unconsciously, the human race is being propelled towards recognising its absolute interconnectedness with the whole.

16

[We] belong to this community of Earth and share in its spectacular self-expression. This is the setting that seems to be implicit in the movements towards ecological integrity in this late 20th century...[10]

It is the special capacity of the human to enable the Universe and the planet Earth to reflect on and to celebrate, not simply the present moment but the total historical process that enables this moment to be what it is.[11]

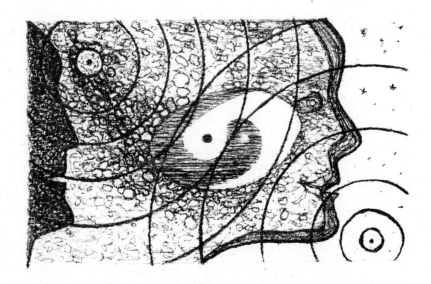

[10] Diarmuid O'Murchu (1996) *The New Cosmology*, (unpublished).
[11] Swimme and Berry (1992) *op. cit.* Epilogue, pp. 264 -7.

3. CHANGING OUR PERCEPTIONS.

> One of the major shifts in consciousness required for our
> time is that we belong to the evolutionary co-creative proc-
> ess, and it is in rediscovering our mutual interdependence...
> that we reclaim our spiritual identity.[12]

The two previous chapters have laid out the background and set
the context from which a Creation Centred Spirituality arises
and presently finds itself. So what is Creation Spirituality?

Spirituality is a human attribute, an innate quality within us
which responds and always has responded to the ultimate
Mystery of Being. Spirituality expresses itself both within and
without formal religion. This expression has had different em-
phases throughout human existence; nevertheless, its core has
always been an awareness of inclusion and interconnectedness,
thus bringing together the bits and pieces which often dominate
our lives, blinding us to their ultimate wholeness. Creation
Spirituality articulates how this innate human spirituality reflects and is immediately 'at home' within the wider understanding of the journey set out in the two previous chapters.

This chapter will describe this response of the spirit to the new
revelation for our time by looking at four dramatic shifts in perception which come from a wider, inclusive vision. Old, deeply
embedded cultural attitudes and assumptions are transformed,
once we look through the wider lens of the new vision. I will
describe in turn a new concept of the sacred; the change from a
human-centred to a cosmic-centred viewpoint; the transformation of the idea of original sin; and finally the healing of the
wounds inflicted by dualistic thinking.

---

[12] Diarmuid O'Murchu (1997) *Reclaiming Spirituality*, Gill and Macmillan,
Ch. 3, p. 41.

18

THE SACRED.

Firstly, then, we can no longer draw a line of distinction between what we consider 'sacred' and what we consider to be 'inanimate matter'. Creation Spirituality sees the whole of creation as sacred. One of the definitions found in the dictionary of the word 'sacred' is 'worthy of, or regarded with reverence and awe.' It is in this sense that the word is used here, thus the reader may fit comfortably anywhere along the spectrum of religious or non-religious belief.

The now undisputed fact that we — the human species and our planet earth — belong within the context of an evolving Universe demands the deepest reverence and awe. Who are we? A Universe that has moved inexorably, over vast unimaginable periods of time from pure energy to matter, and (on this planet) from matter to life, and finally from life to conscious self-awareness, is the milieu in which we now find ourselves. This milieu holds within itself a revelatory new understanding of the place of the human. Within this context the human becomes the self-expression and the self-awareness of the Universe itself. In his book *Reclaiming Spirituality* Diarmuid O'Murchu says:

> The consciousness we possess as human beings... needs to
> be freshly understood as an integral dimension of the intel-
> ligence that permeates all life in the Universe.[13]

And in the words of Matthew Fox, 'Either everything is sacred or nothing is'.

THE COSMOS.

Secondly, we must shift away from our anthropocentrism. Throughout human existence our interpretation of who we are and our relationship with both the created world and the Divine has been entirely from a human-centred perspective. Until now we have known only our own story. With the New Cosmology

---

[13] O'Murchu (1997) *op. cit.* Ch. 6, p. 99.

we find ourselves plunged into a new story, wider, more magnificent, and also more terrifying than any we had previously imagined. Our human-centred viewpoint is now too narrow and too limited for we are part of an ongoing and evolving whole. What changes does this wider cosmic-centred picture make to our understanding of what it is to belong to the human species on planet Earth? I shall mention three.

We have to look again at the value systems by which we order our lives.

Justice, the ecology, even language, need to reflect this new cosmic dimension. For greater detail along these lines see 'Conditions of the Ecozoic Era' in Thomas Berry's *Befriending the Earth*. In his words:

> It is amazing that we should be so sensitive to suicide, homicide, and genocide and have absolutely no moral principles for dealing with biocide or geocide. Over-concerned with the well-being of the human, we feel it is better that everything is destroyed than that humans suffer to any degree.[14]

We are both power-less and power-full

Set against the incomprehensible vastness of the Universe, the human species, living out its short lifespan on planet Earth, can seem ridiculously small and insignificant. Yet the same scenario changes when we recognise that the growth of life and the emergence of consciousness on planet Earth is the one known instance where the universe itself has evolved to a form of conscious self-awareness. Thus the human, with its consciousness and its gift of choice, holds both the power to create and the power to destroy. Paradoxically both views are true.

---

[14] Thomas Berry (1991) *Befriending the Earth*, Twenty-Third Publications. Ch. 4, p. 100.

We are peripheral and we are central

Further, and again paradoxically (for the willingness to embrace paradox is truly a part of this new way of seeing), we are no longer, in the earlier narrow sense, the centre of the Universe. Nevertheless, in the light of our interdependence and interconnectedness within the whole, irrevocably all that we are, do, think or feel affects everything else.

> When we try to pick out anything by itself, we find it hitched to everything else in the Universe...No particle is ever wasted or worn out, but eternally flowing from use to use. [15]

---

[15] Linnie Marsh Wolfe (1973 ed) *John Muir: Son of the Wilderness*, University of Wisconsin Press, p. 123.

The Universe is like a raisin cake in the oven, it expands from every place and angle.[16]

RAISIN CAKE.
If I go anywhere in the Universe,
Southend, The Pleiades, Tierra del Fuego, Mars,
No matter where, it is the same.
I gaze out into 'all that is'
And from that place 'all that is'
Flares outwards.
The expanding Universe blossoms from every point.
Ergo … the centre is everywhere.
Thus … the wild-flower meadow and the dried-out dust-bowl,
The spring-budding chestnut and the felled rain-forest
Are also that centre.
Like a pebble dropped in a pond
All energy, all despair, all beauty, all pain,
All fear, all love, ripples outwards, affects all.
You … me … them … both periphery and centre.

---

[16] Brian Swimme (1991-2). Lecture at The Institute in Culture and Creation Spirituality, Oakland, California.

SIN

The third approach challenges the Christian doctrine of original sin. As Matthew Fox explains in the introduction to his book *Original Blessing*:

> The fall/redemption spiritual tradition is not nearly as ancient as the creation-centred one. The former goes back principally to St Augustine (354 – 430AD)...The Creation Centred tradition traces its roots to the 9th century BC, with the very first author of the Bible, to the Psalms, to the Wisdom books of the Bible, to Jesus, and much of the New Testament.[17]

It cannot be emphasised enough how widely this darkened view of original sin has cast its shadow. We all carry its scars whether Christian or not. Guilt, unworthiness, the rejection of the body as a source of sin, the suppression of spontaneous creativity, all these and more spring from this doctrine which has dominated our western culture for centuries.

A spirituality that is centred in Creation looks to the real beginning, that cloud of shining incandescent radiance, the origin of all that now is. Fifteen billion years later a Creation Centred Spirituality cannot look at the astonishing emergence of a self-aware form of life on this small planet and accept that this particular life-form is singled out to be 'born in sin'. This rejection of the doctrine of original sin does not in any way deny the reality nor the existence of what might be called 'the negative'. There remains an inescapable tension between good and evil, light and dark, creation and destruction. This will be dealt with more fully in the next chapter and reappears under a different guise in the final and fourth look at the shift in perception required in the light of our wider understanding.

---

[17] Matthew Fox (1983) *Original Blessing*, Bear and Co, Introduction, p. 11.

BEYOND DUALISM.

Since Creation Spirituality turns away from a fragmented view of reality to one which embraces the wholeness of creation, there comes a recognition of the rifts that have been created by our dualistic way of describing the world. We see things in terms of opposites and set these opposites in fixed contra-position to each other. Thus, religion is set against science, reason against intuition, the human against the natural world, spirit is seen as opposite of matter, and so on. However, in grasping the concept of the whole we begin to see that these so called opposites are, as it were, the other side of the same thing. Beyond dualism there is the coming together of polarities, the reconciliation of opposites. Instead of either/or there is both/and. These opposites, that our dualistic mode of thinking has made us so comfortable with, turn out to be the necessary co-relatives of each other. As concave and convex, each defines the other, and without the one the other would be unknowable.

> In the beginning there was nothing,
> No-thing — nothing.
> And from the nothing there came
> Longing. A great desire, yearning,
> Yearning for its opposite.
> For in order to define the One
> The existence of the other is necessary.
>
> (From a longer narrative poem *The Story*)

To sum up, it is vitally important that we are aware of the mind-set within which we live, and to recognise how this mind-set has determined cultural attitudes and assumptions. We need to acknowledge also — whether we like it or not — how deeply these assumptions are embedded within our own psyches.

As Einstein is often quoted as saying:

> It is impossible to solve a problem from the same mind-set which created it in the first place.

However, once we can stand back and begin to see things from the new wider perspective, then these old outworn attitudes begin to lose their foothold within our minds. The many-dimensional butterflies of paradox beckon us. Certainty is out — yes. Mystery, challenge, the pain and the wonder of being are ours (as they have always been), but now we know the context and essence of our 'Being'. Our context? A universe emerging into self-awareness. Our 'Being'? An expression of that emergence.

4. THE INSIGHTS OF CREATION SPIRITUALITY.
THE FOUR PATHS.

This chapter will clarify what have come to be known as 'the four paths of Creation Spirituality'. These were first set out by Matthew Fox in his book *Original Blessing*. Primarily they need to be understood as 'enablers'. Enabling us to see through 'different eyes'. 'The eye altering alters all' (William Blake).

> Ideas remain impractical when we have not grasped, or been grasped by them. When we do not get an idea we ask 'how' to put it into practice, thereby trying to turn the insights of the soul into actions of the ego. But when an insight or idea has sunk in, practice invisibly changes. The idea has opened the eye of the soul. By seeing differently we do differently. The only legitimate 'how?' in regard to these psychological insights is: 'How can I grasp an idea'? [18]

> The task is not so much to see what no-one yet has seen, but to think what nobody yet has thought about that which everyone sees.   Schopenhauer.

As these two quotations indicate, our task is to enable these new revelations to bear upon our whole selves, not just upon our intellect so that we can carry 'seeing differently' into all walks of our daily lives.

Creation Spirituality does not lay down rules of 'thou shalt' or 'thou shalt not', instead it offers paths and insights. These spiral from one to the other, enabling a transformed and deeper understanding of what it is to be both an emerging consciousness of an evolving Universe, always in the process of 'becoming', and at the same time, a unique expression and member of the earth community.

---

[18] James Hillman (1992 ed) *Re-visioning Psychology*, Harper Row.

26

THE VIA POSITIVA.

Thou shalt fall in love at least three times a day.[19]

The first path entails re-awakening awe, wonder, astonishment and delight. It has to do with reverence, with 'is-ness', with 'becoming again as little children'.

Forfeit your sense of awe, and the Universe becomes a market place for you. [20]

Is this not exactly what has happened? Could we have ravaged and polluted the planet as we have done if we truly held it and the life it supports in awe? Yet once we have realised the extent of our 'autism', once we have acknowledged how dulled we have allowed our senses to become, it is a small step to begin to see again through the eyes of wonder.

The poet Walt Whitman never lost his sense of the magic and wonder of life, there is nothing to stop us doing the same.

I know nothing else but miracles,
Whether I walk the streets of Manhattan,
Or dart my sight over the roofs of houses towards the
    sky,
Or wade with naked feet along the beach just in the
    edge of the water,
Or stand under trees in the woods,
Or talk by day with anyone I love, or sleep in bed at
    night with anyone I love,
Or sit at table at dinner with the rest,
Or look at strangers opposite me riding in the car,
Or watch honey-bees busy around the hive of a summer
    forenoon,
Or animals feeding in the fields,
Or birds, or the wonderfulness of insects in the air,
Or the exquisite delicate thin curve of the new moon in
    spring,

[19] Matthew Fox (1991) *Creation Spirituality*, Harper San Francisco. p. 19.
[20] Heschel (1955) *God in Search of Man*, New York.

These with the rest, one and all, are to me miracles,
The whole referring, yet each distinct and in its place.
To me every hour of the light and dark is a miracle,
Every square yard of the surface of the earth is spread
    with miracles
Every foot of the interior swarms with miracles. [21]

Annie Dillard, who like Walt Whitman has refused to let go that sense of 'consciously being', speaks of her own awakening, aged five, in her book *An American Childhood*. She says:

> Who could ever tire of this heart-stopping transition, of the breakthrough shift between seeing and knowing you see, between being and knowing you be? [22]

Yet in our culture we often tire very quickly. Our potential to be amazed at 'being' is buried under words, numbers, measurements, explanations.

'Seeing differently' in this respect involves being consciously aware of the deadening effect of the attitude which teaches its young so early to 'take for granted' the moment by moment miracle of 'being'.

The Via Positiva invites us to live our lives open to wonder, to embrace again awe and reverence, to be consciously alive within the present moment…the eternal 'now'. To 'see and to know we see, to be and to know we be'.

---

[21] Walt Whitman (1868 ed) 'Miracles', *Poems by Walt Whitman*, ed. William M Rosssetti, Holten, p 275.
[22] Annie Dillard (1994) 'From an American Childhood', *The Annie Dillard Reader*, Harper Perrenial, p. 140.

THE VIA NEGATIVA.

Embracing the dark. Letting pain be pain.

> I said to my soul — be still
> and let the dark come upon you
> which shall be the darkness of God. [23]

The second path is possibly the most radical in that it takes an alternative route towards understanding and embracing what is described as the 'paradox of good and evil'.

Starting from the wider awareness that the wholeness within which we have our being contains and reconciles all opposites, this path calls us to enter into the pain and the tragedy of existence. Instead of denying the pain and sorrow we allow ourselves to feel and experience it; instead of conquering the darkness by will-power or stoicism, we acknowledge it, living with it and through it.

Embracing the dark, allowing pain to be pain and dark to be dark is not wallowing in misery and being martyrs, neither is it indulging in pessimism, nor is it trying to surmount pain by strength of will and denial.

Yet in the same way our culture distances our sensitivities from wonder and delight, similarly with respect to the dark and negative side of being; rather than face and acknowledge it, we seek to deny it.

Culturally our way of dealing with the darker side of existence follows the path that emerged in the 18th century during that period known as the 'Enlightenment', when we set ourselves to control and defeat nature. We, the human race, will surmount and defeat the pain and struggle of life. Virtually all our western industrial, technological and materialistic society is a reflection of the attitude.

---

[23] T.S.Eliot (1974) 'East Coker', *Collected Poems, 1909-1962*, Faber & Faber.

> Every added protection against the natural world contrib-
> utes its bit to the steadily building illusion of independence
> from nature, so that in time the greatest of illusions is
> erected: the omnipotence of man. [24]

This is a very clear reflection of our western approach and its
consequences; it is not the questioning human spirit that is in
question here but its direction.

If our cultural assumption is that we can defeat and overcome
suffering, then an admission of its reality is seen as failure. The
result of this denial is the 'stiff upper lip' strength of will, the
suppression of the natural expression of grief, and so on. Further results of this denial of the dark side are the ecological dis-
asters that we are causing in our attempts to 'fix the world'.
These results are now coming back to haunt us.

Above all, the Via Negativa is about 'letting go'. Letting go our
desire to control and manipulate, to be 'in charge'.

There is nothing easy about the Via Negativa. It is not a 'spiritual' formula for finding another way to avoid suffering. It is
only possible to move beyond suffering by going through it.
The Via Negativa offers a different kind of strength, a vulnerable
strength that willingly acknowledges the suffering and embraces
it.

'When the heart is broken, compassion can begin to flow'.[25] This
is not a facile statement.

Paradoxically the Via Negativa and the Via Positiva are the Yin
and the Yang, the necessary correlation of each other. The extent
of our willingness to embrace and engage with the darkness is in
direct proportion to our openness to awe, wonder and delight.
Moreover, to the extent that we deny the reality that wholeness

---

[24] Frederick Turner (1992) *Beyond Geography: the Western Spirit Against the
Wilderness*, Rutgers University Press.
[25] Matthew Fox (1987) *The Four Paths of Creation Spirituality.* St. James's
Church.

includes both dark and light, both pain and joy, to that extent we
diminish and undermine our own spiritual growth.

> Man was made for joy and woe
> And when this we rightly know
> Through the world we safely go.[26]

LET THE DARK BE DARK.

> The old voices kept insisting
> Make up your mind
> Now.
> Refuse to suffer,
> Indecision is weak,
> Not knowing is a dumb game.
> But the new voice whispered . . .
> Wait . . .
> Stay in the darkness.
> It will enclose you as velvet,
> Embrace the pain,
> For it is a necessity of new birth.
> And do not reject 'not knowing'
> For to stand humbly with
> Uncertainty
> Is both trust and wisdom.
> The answer will come in its own time . . .
> Not yours.

There is, however, a darker side, which it requires all our wisdom and courage to recognise. It springs directly out of the
great venture of the universe — moving as it has towards con-

---

[26] William Blake (1989 ed) 'Auguries of Innocence' in *Blake: the Complete Poems*, ed. W.H. Stevenson, Longmans, p. 589.

sciousness — for contained within that lies the human gift of choice. Thus our human desire to avoid the dark and pain has also given rise to the pursuit of power over others. This has resulted in the devaluation and abuse of human by human. Here then is a subversion of the true Via Negativa and we need to recognise and acknowledge it.

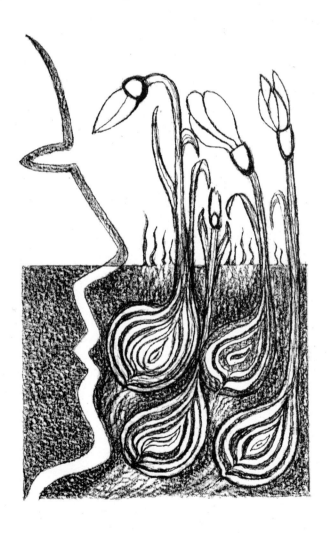

THE VIA CREATIVA.

Expressing our own true selves.

> You must give birth to your images. They are the future waiting to be born...Fear not the strangeness you feel. The future must enter into you long before it happens. [27]

> The Universe has unfolded to this point. It has poured into you the creative powers necessary for its further development. The journey of the Cosmos depends upon those creatures and elements existing now, you among them. For the unfolding of the Universe your creativity is as essential as the creativity inherent in the fireball. [28]

The third path calls us to connect again with that creative power which already dwells within us, yet, as with so much else that was once spontaneous, our culture has numbed us to its voice by imposing a narrow definition of what is and what is not 'creative'. Most people, by the time they reach the adult world have lost touch with, as well as confidence in, their inner creative energy.

Yet this is a terrible denial of the reality of who we are; each one a unique expression of that sacred energy which unfolds itself in never ending abundance.

Trusting in that creativity which is in each of us does not mean we should all become painters, musicians or poets, but what it does mean is that we will learn again to trust our deepest feelings. It will mean giving birth to ideas and imagination, play and surprise, boldness and intuition.

In the words of Rainer Maria Rilke — yes, the future must enter into us before it happens, and that future will be formed by how

---

[27] Rainer Maria Rilke (2000 ed) *Letters to a Young Poet*, trans. Joan M Burnham. Ingram, Letter 3.
[28] Brian Swimme (1984) *The Universe is a Green Dragon*, Bear & Co. p 29.

these dreams and visions within us are either listened to and honoured, or ignored.

Suppressing the natural creative energy within a person will result in it returning thwarted, in a more destructive guise.

'Do you create, or do you destroy?' asked Dag Hammarskjold.

We cannot be neutral.

The greatest and most important thing we can do with our lives is to be who we truly are. But unless we pay attention to allowing that creative energy which is within us to express itself, then it will never be seen. There is no duplication; we are, each one of us 'one-off's'! As every leaf and every blade of grass is unrepeatable, so are we.

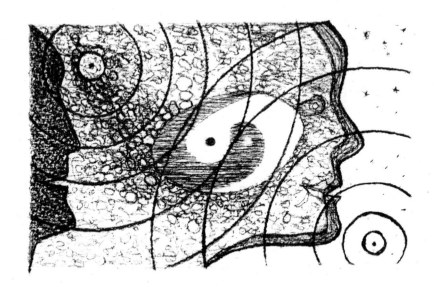

34

The quotation used by Nelson Mandela in his inaugural speech is addressed to every member of the human race.

Our deepest fear
is not that we are inadequate.
Our deepest fear
is that we are powerful beyond measure.
It is our light,
not our darkness,
that most frightens us.
We ask ourselves,
who am I to be brilliant,
gorgeous, talented, fabulous?
Actually, who are you not to be?
You are a child of God.
Your playing small doesn't serve the world.
There's nothing enlightened about shrinking
so that other people
won't feel insecure around you.
We were born to make manifest
the glory of God that is within us.
It's not just in some of us;
it's in everyone.
And as we let our own light shine,
we unconsciously give other people
permission to do the same.
As we are liberated from our own fear,
our presence automatically liberates others. [29]

---

[29] Marianne Williamson (1992) *A Return to Love*, Harper Collins.

THE VIA TRANSFORMATIVA.

Embracing Compassion, Justice and Wisdom.

> Nothing has changed, except the way I see things — and so
> everything has changed. (Author unknown.)

The fourth path, named the Via Transformativa, brings the insights of compassion, justice and wisdom to bear upon our interpretation of the previous three paths, most particularly upon that of the Via Creativa. 'Do we create or do we destroy?' asked Dag Hammerskjold. Our creativity will need the compassionate direction of wisdom and justice, for we are not puppets. We are a species with self-awareness, a species that knows it knows, a species with the power to choose.

Our conditioning is deep however, and we slip back into old patterns of seeing so easily. Yet each small illumination, each seemingly slight shift in perception is a step along the way of our Cosmic unfolding.

I want in this final path to name five subtle transformations in perception that will mark our journey as the new vision of who we are dawns upon us.

From consumer to partaker.

As the new story penetrates our consciousness we see ourselves no longer as consumers but as partakers. A consumer devours without thought or consideration — as we currently devour and consume the precious life-sustaining systems of our planet. A partaker starts from a different viewpoint. A partaker shares, aware of mutual interdependence, a partaker takes only what is fair and just.

From observer to participant.

We are not detached observers in an inanimate world, which is the predominantly held view in our current western attitude towards life on this planet. However much we may prefer to be detached, we are not. The awareness of our total dependence upon our planet and our interconnectedness, will transform us from detached observers to participants. A participant, as with a partaker, comes from within, not without, as a member of the earth community. Active, responsible, compassionate, and involved.

From Tourists to Pilgrims.

> Put off thy shoes from off thy feet, for the place whereon thou standest is holy ground. (Exodus 3:5.)

A pilgrim is one who recognises and seeks the sacred. The vision here is that of Creation Spirituality, which views the whole of creation as sacred, i.e. worthy of reverence and awe. Within the attitude of the 'pilgrim' seeking and recognising the 'sacred' there comes an enrichment, an enhancement of both 'parties'. (Try it and see)! The tourist, on the other hand, is concerned with superficialities, a detached visitor to the planet, unconcerned with deeper meanings.

From Masters to Co-Creators, and from Doers to Listeners.

Both of these shifts acknowledge the reality that we, as humans, are not 'in control'. Yet our role — as the conscious self-awareness of the evolving earth-community — is far from a passive one; it calls us to embrace our cosmic destiny as active participants in the great unfolding. No longer an embattled species in an alien world, we see ourselves as responsible co-creators, using all our wisdom and compassion to work with, and not against, nature.

We now face our greatest challenge, how do we exercise that gift of self-conscious awareness that is ours?

It is we who are alive today who have the responsibility of guiding this species on. It is we who have to find ways to release ourselves to the full significance of the present time.[30]

The reader can easily recognise that each one of these four paths points to nothing more nor less than 'a different way of seeing'. Nothing has changed except that we now know where we truly belong. That we are inextricably a part of a cosmic evolution, which here and now on a small planet on the edge of the Milky Way has blossomed into consciousness. We are that blossoming. We are the Universe aware of itself.

We may choose to consider the dawn of consciousness as 'pure chance' or as 'pre-ordained'; the responsibility upon the human as the beneficiary of that awareness remains the same.

'What is the human?' asks Brian Swimme. 'The human is a space, an opening, where the Universe celebrates its existence'. [31]

Each path weaves in and out of the others, each enhances and supports the others. Primarily, as stated at the start of this chapter, they are 'enablers' enabling us to see differently, thus becoming conscious participants in the unfolding of the great Cosmic Symphony in which every note counts.

> Because you are aware of the limits of life, you are com-pelled to bring forth what is within you; this is the only time you have to show yourself. You can't hold back or hide in a cave,... the drama of the Cosmic story won't allow it. The supreme insistence of life is that you enter the ad-venture of creating yourself. [32]

---

[30] Peter Russell (1992) *A White Hole in Time*, Harper San Francisco, p. 224.

[31] Swimme (1984) *op. cit.* p. 146.

[32] Swimme (1984) *op. cit.* p. 117.

5. THE INCLUSIVE JOURNEY.

An acknowledgement of the world's varied belief systems and their place within the 'New Story'.

> Nor is it the case that this story suppresses the other stories that have over the millennia guided and energised the human venture. It is rather a case of providing a more comprehensive context in which all these earlier stories discover for themselves a new validity, and a more expansive role. [33]

In many respects this chapter might be seen as a continuation of chapter 1, which attempted to show how the emerging human consciousness sought to explain and find answers to the mystery of existence.

Out of this human quest have arisen what may loosely be called the 'great religions' as well as the native spiritualities. Teilhard de Chardin in his comprehensive story of the evolving universe (*The Phenomenon of Man*), shows its development to be both psychic and material, i.e. both spiritual and physical. In the same way that every living form that has emerged since the dawning of the Universe is an integral part of that emergence, so too is every new insight, every intimation of our deep interconnectedness, every vision of our human destiny. Thus we must embrace the recognition that the emergence of the differing religions is an equally valid part of the ongoing but unfinished journey of human consciousness within the evolving Universe.

It is not the purpose of this chapter to analyse and define the deep insights pertaining to each individual religious revelation. The meaning of the word 'revelation' given in the dictionary is 'the act or process of disclosing something previously secret or obscure, especially something true'. It is in this sense that I use the word here. Thus the new understanding brought to us through science is equally a revelation, previously unknown but nevertheless true.

---

[33] Swimme and Berry (1992) *op. cit.* p 238.

> I consider that our new understanding of the Universe is a
> new revelatory experience…it is the way the divine is pres-
> ently revealing itself to us. [34]

Over the centuries the world's religions have accumulated much
in the way of 'clutter', some valuable, some not. However, when
we look with the eyes of wisdom at the simple revelation in the
original message, we will recognise, without exception, that the
underlying message offers an illumination, opening up a shaft of
light upon our understanding of the nature of the Ultimate Reality, God, the Ground of our Being, or whatever name the
reader feels most comfortable with.

The time-developmental evolutionary Universe within which
we now see ourselves poses no threat, anymore than did the
revelation mentioned earlier when the only change forced upon
us by the fact that the sun did not orbit the earth as we had sup-
posed, but the earth orbited the sun, was a widening of the context within which we interpreted the world and our place in it.

Similarly today, it is only our understanding of the context of
our being that is being challenged.

> There is always the mystery of things, and the mystery of
> existence can be given the name divine, it can be called God,
> or immanence, or whatever one wishes, we must admit the
> mystery of things. [35]

And the 'mystery of things' in this new and wider context is that
we are a part of an unfolding that is greater and more mysterious that we had ever imagined.

As Swimme and Berry point out in the quotation at the start of
this chapter, all human insights and revelations which have
guided the human venture are inextricably themselves a valid
part of the ongoing unfolding.

---

[34] Berry (1991) *op. cit.* p 16.
[35] Berry (1991) *op. cit.* p 19.

So our challenge now is to find that 'more expansive role'. Trusting that deep intuitive knowing that is ours we shall be enabled to let fall away the impedimenta and clutter that have accumulated over the centuries within our chosen spiritual path, and embrace again the profound insights which lie at the centre of each one of these revelations. For it is within these understandings and perceptions that the new validity, and the more expansive role lie.

Faith and doubt are not polar opposites; to trust one's uncertainty needs courage. This is the sort of faith which trusts itself to a venture so awe-inspiringly vast, that its unfolding to the here and now has taken 12 billion years. Yet that small act of faith, in itself, becomes a contribution and a reinforcement of that very unfolding. A human expression of the consciousness of the Universe becomes an integral part of that unfolding. Everything, spiritual and material, is a part of the whole.

CREATION SPIRITUALITY IN THE UK.

Creation Spirituality is a movement, not a belief or an organisation. So in the UK its ideas bubble up in many forms, through organisations with many names. This pamphlet comes from GreenSpirit (the Association for Creation Spirituality) which provides opportunities for finding out more about the movement. We conclude with a brief historical sketch.

The name, in the form "Creation Centered Spirituality", was first coined by Matthew Fox, and expounded in *Original Blessing* and other books. His vision, whilst springing from the Christian tradition — built on the Jewish conception of the world as the fundamental revelation of God, and of eco-justice as fulfilment of that revelation — nevertheless also embraces the new cosmology and science. The Centre for Creation Spirituality was set up at St James's Church, Piccadilly, London, as a result of four talks Matthew Fox was invited to give at St James's in 1987. A follow-up meeting had resulted in local groups being started, and the need for a focal point then became clear, both as a central contact place as well as a means of providing contact between groups. This centre was started on a voluntary basis by Petra Griffiths, first from her own home, and later from St James's itself when Donald Reeves, the rector, agreed to provide an office base.

By the end of 1989, and helped by volunteers, Petra became the first paid co-ordinator for the centre. A regular newsletter listing events around the country was produced, and the C.S. Journal 'Interchange' was launched. Later, introductory courses were run by John Doyle and Madelaine O'Callaghan, both graduates of Matthew Fox's Institute in Culture and Creation Spirituality. In addition, a link was forged with Birkbeck College Extra-Mural Studies Department and courses were run there by John Doyle until he returned to Ireland.

In 1990 Alan Shephard set up his Creation Spirituality mail order book service. This provided — and provides — an immense panorama of reading matter, bringing together Spirituality and

Ecology, Poetry and Local Economics, Native Wisdom and New Cosmology — and much more. This service has changed its name to *GreenSpirit Books*, and since 1999 includes the Schumacher Book Service. Profits are donated to GreenSpirit.

In 1994 the organisation applied to the Charity Commissioners for charitable status, and became The Association for Creation Spirituality, an Unincorporated Membership Organisation, with Jane Horton as co-ordinator and Ingrid Hankins as administrator, working with a Council whose members hold legal responsibility for the Charity.

After this a succession of changes transformed the organisation into its current form. The "public name" of GreenSpirit was adopted in 1997. Funding by St James's was progressively phased out as the organisation learnt to stand on its own feet, and moved to a more voluntary basis. The previous publications *Interchange* and *Newsletter* were merged to the single journal *GreenSpirit*, which has become the main means by which the local groups maintain contact with each other and with the wider Creation Spirituality movement. Much of the administrative work, the writing and editing of this pamphlet, and the editing and graphics of the Journal is done voluntarily, mostly by Council members, and paid work is kept to a minimum.

Each local group is entirely independent, and their different approaches cover a broad spectrum. Through its groups this movement seeks to rediscover a lost sense of interconnectedness and belonging, and at the same time to widen this sense to embrace the new knowledge of our place in the ongoing story. Thus in order to be in touch with the seasons and the spirit of local places of Britain, several groups build their programme around celebrations of the traditional eight festivals of the Celtic year. Others draw from a variety of spiritual traditions, including some practices of the indigenous American nations, while yet others draw mainly from the Christian tradition. The styles of meetings are equally varied, covering talks, discussions, video showings, meditations, artistic creativity, circle dancing or free dancing, drumming, ritual ... Many groups have some meetings outdoors or on traditional sacred sites.

As well as networking these groups and putting enquirers in contact with them, GreenSpirit organises larger national events, such as visits by major international speakers, courses and retreats on Creation Centred Spirituality, or extended workshops on key topics. It maintains a Web site (see below) which is developing into a resource centre and news centre, and also provides access to the book service and facilities for joining Green-Spirit.

GreenSpirit now looks forward to continued growth in numbers, and continued flourishing of its local and national activities. While offering much to those working for renewal within the Christian Church, the breadth of vision upon which it rests offers an authentic spiritual home to many from differing spiritual paths or from none. Through its work more and more people share ways of discovering and celebrating the richness of our world, and join in the adventure of being co-creators in an on-going transformation of themselves, of society, and of the planet.

To join or find out more, contact GreenSpirit at

Tel: 020 7287 2741
        Centre for Creation Spirituality, St
        James's Church,
        197 Piccadilly, London, W1J 9LL
Web: http://www.greenspirit.org.uk

FURTHER READING.

Thomas Berry (1999) *The great work*. Bell Tower.

Matthew Fox (1983) *Original Blessing*. Bear and Co.

Brian Swimme and Thomas Berry (1992) *The Universe Story*. Harper San Francisco.